When Everything Comes From NOTHINGNESS

Julius Ferner jun.

An Illusionistic View of the World

When Everything Comes From
NOTHINGNESS

Bibliographic Information of the Deutsche Nationalbibliothek:
The German National Library has registered this publication in the German National Bibliography;
detailed bibliographic information can be found on the Internet at http://dnb.d-nb.de.

© 2016 Julius Ferner jr.
Typesetting, cover design, production and publishing house:
BoD – Books on Demand
ISBN: 978-3-7392-9937-2

An Illusionistic View of the World

When Everything Comes From Nothingness

Can everything come from NOTHINGNESS?

That is a question philosophers and scientists have been racking their brains over for centuries and they still have no answer. Yet, there is definitely an answer to the question:

It is only from NOTHINGNESS that everything can evolve!

Any other premise for the origin of our universe would have prevented all the options available to us from developing in the first place. That is because options allow for a positive and a negative answer to everything. A fixed premise would exclude the possibility of a negative. With the exception of NOTHINGNESS, where the very essence of the negative makes everything possible.
At the same time, this also means:

Absolute freedom can only come from NOTHINGNESS!

That is because absolute freedom only exists if one can choose from everything. It thus follows that:

Love can only grow out of NOTHINGNESS!

Love without freedom of choice is not love, it is merely a programmed event or a dictate.

As a result, NOTHINGNESS is also an imperative condition for freedom and for love.
 Is there anything more important to the human race than freedom and love?

The question as to "Why does everything even exist?" is as old as humanity itself. Attempts to answer it have thus led to various ways of viewing the world. To be exact, there are as many views of the world as there are heads in the world; among the seven billion people alive, no two share the same level of information. However, there are larger and smaller groups who tend to think along similar lines. One thing holds true for each of them: they all believe, but do not know. Even professionals of the natural sciences – with science itself being defined as a body or branch of knowledge – are merely a community of believers, although no comparison or degradation is intended here.

One characteristic common among all world views is the presumption of a condition, an original force, behind the existence of their universe, whether in the form of a god, different gods, god-like powers, universal energy, ideas, matter, etc. The problem with such communities of believers lies in the fact that they lack evidence to support the origins of their presumed conditions. For example, one could even assume the creator or original force to be either the devil or a collective power of all black holes or any other concept one might find appealing. Furthermore, any one of them could be correct, as none can prove the existence of their original force nor do they need to fear anyone providing evidence that would disprove their original force.

Is there any faith that does not face this problem?
Is there a faith that does not need a fixed premise?

Toward the end of his life, poet Christian Morgenstern (1871-1914) is allegedly reported to have replied as follows to the question of the purpose of life, "Life is NOTHINGNESS' search for something."
A fantastic answer. He sees himself as the personification of NOTHINGNESS.

The English bishop and philosopher George Berkley (1685-1753) was of the conviction that all material objects, including time and space, were merely an illusion. He even went so far as to express this conviction to Isaac Newton; although at the time, Newton was famous and untouchable with his laws of motion, which showed how matter reacted to forces.

In Buddhism there is also a school of thought, which calls itself "Cittamatra", whose position is that the material world, including time and space, is merely an illusion.

Quantum physics discusses the question of whether material objects exist if the sensory organs cannot register them as such.

In 2006, a professor of physics, the producer of a popular scientific television series in Germany, titled one of his episodes, "Why isn't there nothing?". As a materialist, he was surprised that matter existed. He could not understand where it came from. Naturally, he was unable to answer the question of that episode's title. His question had, however, hit the nail on the head: The only belief that does not require a premise is the belief in NOTHINGNESS. Or, to put it more clearly, because we are not nothing: the belief that everything comes from NOTHINGNESS, that everything simply exists in our heads and is thus a mere illusion.

What exactly is illusion?

The Brockhaus encyclopedia describes illusion as a "self deception or false interpretation of sensations or a pseudo-reality created by special means".

Accordingly, an illusion is created when information we perceive through our senses is processed in our brain and causes one or a few or many living creatures to believe in a reality that does not actually exist.

Here are a few well-known examples: The Fata Morgana, which makes an oasis and water appear to be close by in the desert, even though both are an unreachable distance away.

Or the Ptolemaic view of the world, which was considered reality by the majority of humankind for approximately 1,400 years and which considers the earth to be center of the universe, with everything rotating around it, even the sun and the other stars.

One particularly impressive and current example are computer programs, which can provide a realistic display of almost all aspects of our world, even though they are merely a programmed sequence of information consisting of zeros and ones. We perceive living creatures, objects, actions, spaces and the passing of time, even though the only thing that actually exists besides a two-dimensional screen is bits. In other words, a sequence of binary signals can present an illusion of reality.

This fact by itself is rather astonishing, but what is even more astounding is the very short amount of time in which it developed, namely about fifty years. The digital principle of information shaping and information processing seems to be embedded in the human mind.

Is it impossible that fifteen billion years of evolution will have created a perfect illusion of all aspects of life?

What do we mean by reality?

One reality that is very simple and free of doubt, is for example, a pebble. Our eyes see a light or dark gray stone shimmering in the bed of a river; it has been worn smooth and is about the size of the palm of your hand. We pick it up and register its solid, round form that has been worn smooth. It is so solid and hard, that it hurts when it falls on our foot.

Does this one-hundred-percent reality hold up under the scrutiny of a single test?

What is the pebble made of? Primarily of a compound of the element of silicon with other elements, such as hydrogen, oxygen or even metals. All elements, as well as other matter, plants, animals or people, consist of atoms. All atoms are more than 99.99 percent empty, the rest we refer to as the atomic nucleus and electrons. What does that mean for our pebble? If reduced to an atomic nucleus and electrons, it would no longer be visible to us.

To be precise, our eyes do not actually see a pebble either. What reaches our eyes, after all, is daylight reflected off the pebble (or whatever it happens to be) in very specific wavelengths, which our brain interprets as gray to dark gray. The form of the pebble is created by setting it apart from its surroundings: the other pebbles next to it or even the aquatic plants being moved by the current. The same holds true here as well, our eyes are merely receiving daylight reflected off the other pebbles. This gives them shape, and the area where the pebbles touch appears to have a darker edge, but here little or no light is reflected. The plants reflect other wavelengths, which our brain automatically interprets as green or brown, for example. Even their form is determined by the light of other wavelengths that is reflected by the objects around them.

If we hold the pebble in our hand, we can feel the hardness of it. Just how little this feeling of resistance must have with the reality of matter can be seen when we attempt to put two magnets with the same poles together. We cannot do it, even though the only thing between the two is air.

If our brain can display different wavelengths of light as color or shape, it is certainly able to interpret this resistance as a hard matter.

Ultimately, the reality of the pebble has less to do with its color, shape or hardness and more to with how our brain interprets information as matter.

When the Greek philosopher Democritus founded the teaching of atoms around 2,500 years ago, he said, "An entity only appears to have a color, it only appears to be sweet or bitter, when in reality, it is only atoms and empty space."

Yet, the empty space does not exist either, as none has yet discovered the limits of our universe. A space without limits is not a space. Thus, there are only atoms and NOTHINGNESS. Accordingly, space is a belief. The same holds true for time. We try to establish a sense of order in our microscopically small phase of life by defining the rotation of the earth around its own axis as day and night, one-twenty-fourth of that as an hour and so on and so forth. When we realized that this type of time measurement was neither generally valid nor consistent, as each planet has a different speed of rotation, which happens to be constantly changing, we had to come up with another way to measure time.

How do we currently measure time and space that does not exist? We measure them with atoms or atomic particles, with the oscillation of the cesium atom or with the speed of light.

What are atoms?

As mentioned above, an atom consists of 99.99 percent of NOTHING. There is no knowledge about the rest as yet, merely newer and newer hypotheses of varying atomic models. The progress made over the last few thousand years consists in having split the previously indivisible (old Greek: Atomos) into an atomic nucleus and electrons. The atomic nucleus was then smashed, first into a few, then into many particles. The model currently accepted by many physicists, the string theory, suggests the string to be the smallest particle. The string is supposedly shaped like a crooked worm, almost reminding one of a deformed bit, similar to a sinus curve. The estimated, unimaginable tininess of a string can only be vaguely illustrated by a comparison: If we were able to blow an invisible atom up to the size of the globe, this string would be the size of a single eyelash on that globe!

Thus, physics is actually quite close to proving NOTHINGNESS. If we venture a small step further by claiming that a string is not material either, and if we take into consideration the fact that our sensory organs and our brain also consist of atoms, we can only come to the conclusion that which we consider reality is simply our illusionistic unit's – that being the brain – interpretation of our illusionistic environment – that being our universe. The result cannot be reality.

This inevitably leads to the following question at this point: If everything we consider to be our universe, including ourselves, is actually a mere illusion, then what is reality?

Before we attempt to answer this question, we should examine the consequences an illusionistic view of the world, meaning the development of everything from NOTHINGNESS, would have for the human race.

Objection By a Competent Buddhist

During a discussion with leading quantum physicists, the Dalai Lama allegedly made the following point regarding this topic: "To me personally, the ideas behind an illusionistic view of the world seems rather untenable from a philosophical point of view. They provide no answers to the questions: What helps us and what harms us? How can we lessen our greed and our hatred and do away with them in the end?"

In this case, however, the Dalai Lama – a recipient of the Nobel Peace Prize and one of the few reasonable people in the world with some authority – is wrong. That is because a more extensive examination of the ethical values of an illusionistic ideology would show that it does hold the potential to resolve the problems he mentioned, something it seems the current bodies of believers are not in a position to do.

The Dalai Lama considers greed and hatred primarily to be human problems. The daily overflow of information on how people are treating one another, treating animals, plants and other natural resources, seems to confirm his claim. Thus, it would be worthwhile to clarify the root of these two feelings and why they are so powerful.

The evolution of these feelings started no later than with the beginning of life, when molecules managed to separate themselves from other particles by means of a membrane and to form the first single-celled organisms.

Their biggest problem was survival. From that point on,

they had to make positive and negative decisions: Which particles do I let in or collect that are critical to my survival and which harmful ones do I need to fend off or flee from? These were decisions that every life form that evolved had to make, whether bacteria, plants, fungus, animals or people, and make in a split second in order to survive. That is also why throughout evolution, they became automatic, conditioned decisions which presented themselves as emotions. From this, we can derive that the development of emotions was a necessity for our survival. Meaning, the ability to react immediately, without reflection, as soon as we receive information. This applies in equal measure for both positive and negative feelings. As a result, evaluating our feelings as good or bad contradicts their evolutionary significance. A negative feeling toward an enemy is just as important to our survival as the positive is toward a friend.

Brain research has shown that most of the decisions we consider to be conscious were already pre-made by our emotions. That explains the immense influence our emotions have on our lives. This is reinforced by the fact that a negative (not necessarily bad) feeling automatically leads to hostile thought and action, while a positive feeling causes affirmative thought and action.

Why then are hatred and greed two negative feelings that appear to be destroying our world, but have been activated to ensure our survival?

Hatred arises when our own sovereignty is continuously disregarded by our fellow humans. Greed results from a desire for more attention and respect. If we understand attention to be respect or as an aspect of love, then hatred and greed indicate an acute deficit in attention and love. The rational reasons as to why our emotions are right are obvious:

1.0. Most bodies of believers suggest there is an omnipotent power that created everything, including humans. The individual considers themselves a small part of a mass production and must submit to the guidelines of their own community of believers. In doing so, they feel neither respected nor loved, but dependent and meaningless instead.

2.0. How humans deal with their negative emotions – they are deemed bad, rejected and suppressed – even though they serve the purpose of survival.
2.1. By doing so, humans reject a part of themselves, since
2.2. their personality is the result of their emotions, thoughts and actions. How can they respect or love others, when they are forced to reject themselves? They are unable to love themselves and thus are unable to love their fellow humans.
2.3. Naturally, they are free to love themselves when they do good.
Yet, that is only true of part of their life.

3.0. This weakened sense of self-worth is replaced with competition, which becomes almost like a drug. Competition between people and in every aspect of their lives. Humans attempt to improve their feeling of self-worth by comparing themselves to others with the goal of being better than others. This leads to a sense of self-righteousness, dismissiveness towards others, fraud, exploitation and abuse of power. Greed is the quest to be "better" than others. Its tools are exploitation and abuse of power. The result is hatred from those who suffer from it.

These are three profound causes that lead to the suppression of a strong self-worth and thus love as well.

The Consequences of an Illusionistic View of the World

If the universe and humans arose out of NOTHINGNESS, then, logically, they must have set out on the path of evolution themselves. This, in turn, would force the following consequences:

Consequence A

We are free to think, feel and act, as there is no higher authority. Our thoughts, emotions and actions developed of their own accord as part of evolution. According to biologists and brain researchers, all restrictions and compulsions, such as conditioning, emotions, genes and body, do not affect our freedom, as we shaped them ourselves for reasons of survival. It is up to us to abolish them when it is necessary.

Consequence B

We alone are responsible for our past, present and future. We created everything and are now the only force that effectuates things. There is no other power. Everything is our common creation. We even developed our communities of faith ourselves. Together, we can change anything that displeases us today.

So, what does it mean to assume responsibility for the past and the present?

It means saying "Yes" to everything we are in the present moment, without restriction. Saying "Yes" to everything that is, including our fears, which we have learned to see as something negative, something to be denied and suppressed. Saying "Yes" to our fears does not have to be hard if we take into consideration that fear activates our instinct for survival when we recognize danger. Fear causes us to take measures necessary for our survival.

Consequence C

We ourselves hold the power that created and creates everything, as there is no other force. As each individual represents a part of everything that exists, than each individual holds the energy that effectuates everything.

Is that possible, probable or even realistic?

Numerous, highly intelligent people have already racked their brains trying to figure out why some people achieve everything, while others do not. Innumerable books exist on the topic.

The authors include world-famous motivational gurus who are convinced that people can achieve anything they really set their minds to. They all come to the same conclusion: The instrument of power they all strive for is emotion, stimulated by our imagination and convictions. The condition for achieving target results? The repetitive visualization of the goals over an extended period, which must go hand in hand with a strong feeling of joy, love, fear or hatred.

Even the Old Testament states that faith can move

mountains. But what is faith if not imagination combined with a sense of certainty? All miracles that have occurred can be attributed to those factors. This instrument of power we have works thousand-fold and in every area of our lives, and an individual's genes, origin, education or training is irrelevant.

The considerable impact that emotions can have, whether positive or negative, has already been seen. Just think about Jesus of Nazareth, Buddha, Mahatma Gandhi, Adolf Hitler, Josef Stalin, Albert Schweitzer, Mother Theresa and so many others.

This leads to the conclusion: We hold the power not to fight the feelings of greed and hatred, but to recognize wherein they are rooted and to realize Consequence D.

Consequence D

Freedom and responsibility apply to every single one of us under consideration of the sovereignty of the individual. Everyone is part of everything that exists. Everyone consists of the same material as everything around them. Everyone is equipped with the same energy found in everything else.

If each of us embodies part of the whole and one of us acts against another, then that person is actually acting against part of themselves and thus against themselves. Anytime one of us advocates on another's behalf, we are also fostering our own well-being.

The same naturally applies for respect and rejection. We are all familiar with the great feeling of bringing joy to someone and the bad feeling of doing something mean. After all, neighborly love is a logical consequence of the illusionistic world view. It already manifests itself in our emotions.

Consequence E

If we have evolved from NOTHINGNESS, then polarity is a prerequisite. The logical principles of mathematics apply if we equate NOTHINGNESS with zero. Zero is always the result of the sum of equal polar values, for example: 1 and -1, yes and no, + the root of 5 / − the root of 5, etc.

As a result, polarity is the precondition for our existence; thus, for our universe. The laws of nature and energy are consequences of polarity. Even humans are the personification of polarity: each of our innumerable atoms of which we consist has a positive and a negative charge.

In an illusionistic view of the world, humans can only love their negative emotions as without them, they could not exist for two reasons:

1. Nothing would exist without polarity

2. Evolution would not have been possible without negative emotions as they help us survive

If a human were to consequently view their negative emotions with love, they would become love.

If we assume that the human is now aware of what a miracle it is to have evolved from NOTHINGNESS and to be able to experience everything, they would no longer be faced with question of the meaning or purpose of life. The only alternative to being is NOTHINGNESS, to which they can return at any time should they wish.

Furthermore, when a person realizes they have achieved everything by themselves, then it follows that they must love themselves!

If they are also able accept the fact that everything that is negative is necessary for their very existence, then they will be happy!

How could everything come from NOTHINGNESS?

What is NOTHINGNESS?

It is not something we can imagine. It cannot be described. Yet, it can be defined: NOTHINGNESS is a state in which nothing exists. This state is, however, extremely labile. It is a paradox: If nothing exists then NOTHINGNESS cannot exist either. Meaning, that everything is possible as well. This constant contradiction is equivalent to the continuous information of 0, 1, 0, 1, 0, 1, etc. In turn, this means that there could have been a state of awareness in the simplest form even before the big bang:

NOTHINGNESS or not NOTHINGNESS (= everything).

The number of bits per second under an oscillation frequency of 0, 1 would be at least 10 to the 15th power if we base it on that of light. As there is no space in NOTHINGNESS, the oscillations could not leave or exit the NOTHINGNESS. This could cause them to rotate, which would prevent equalization and generate polarity.

The continuous information of 0, 1 and the increasing rotation and polarization stabilization affiliated with it could have created the conditions that produced the big bang with enough bits for a digital display of the entire universe.

According to the discoveries of physics, the big bang must have been an explosion of unimaginable strength. Yet, instead of matter creating space in the form of atoms and atomic particles, it brought awareness (units of information) in varying complexities including information about space. Resulting, physicists believe, in the creation of sixty-one physical atomic particles with different shapes and functions. These particles could also be considered units of information formed and merged by the explosion and consisting of many bits with different informational content. Thus, for example, an atom could be a complex unit of information consisting of innumerable bits and containing information on space and anti-space that physicians call gravitation, as well as other information, such as electrostatic attraction and resistance, and representing NOTHINGNESS and everything. The information of NOTHINGNESS and everything, of 1 and 0, is found in even the smallest unit of information. It was the birth of awareness even before the big bang and became, through innumerable repetitions, reality. Today still, we talk about reality when events repeat themselves. The more frequent the repetition, the more the event is accepted as reality.

Which is why it is no surprise that from the very start, the battle of realities – of everything or NOTHINGNESS – determined how our universe evolved. With that evolution taking place even in the subatomic, atomic and molecular field, it had only one goal, namely that of accomplishing a labile state of NOTHINGNESS, of everything or nothing. The more information that was found in a unit, the greater its chance of survival was (knowledge is power). However, with that grew the probability of vulnerability. Within itself, an atom held sixty-one times as much information as an elementary particle. A heavy atom had many more functions than, for example, a hydrogen atom. Molecules, in turn, were superior to an atom in regard to information and function. Molecules became cells, which were able to reproduce. Cells became plants, which generated their own energy for survival. Thus, the evolution of everything continued from bacteria to fungus to animals, and finally, to humans.

Our universe consists exclusively of units of information, which we could also call awareness with varying degrees of complexity, regardless of whether we not refer to it as matter, plant or animal.

On earth, humans are the awareness with the most highly and well organized units of information. It is an awareness of the greatest complexity (knowledge is power). At the same time, it also has the greatest vulnerability. The touch of a button would suffice to extinguish humanity. The human being is not matter; it is mere information and information processing. It simply represents a unit of well-coordinated organizations composed of units of information consisting of bits. All of the images it sees of itself and its world are merely illusions, produced by its information processing center, its brain. All of its actions are virtual. All of its friends and its suffering are things it has created itself in collaboration with its fellow humans and its environment. Even its environment exists exclusively of units of information that exchange information, among themselves, meaning it too is simply awareness. Life and death are illusions. They are creations of the brain. The human is part of everything, and thus part of NOTHINGNESS, and, in the exchange between the two, experiences a fantastic adventure. Time and again! Without cease! It does so with freedom, love and responsibility for itself.

Yet, this whole theory about NOTHINGNESS and the illusionistic world view is mere speculation, right?

Right! It is as much pure speculation as those shared by bodies of believers, including those who consider matter to be reality. Yet, it gives us with one decisive difference:

It is the speculation about an unimaginable NOTHINGNESS alone that gives humans permission to realize their ideals, freedom, love and self-responsibility.
 Is there a higher purpose?
 Is that purpose not self-evident?